I want to be a
BASKETBALL
PLAYER

By Eugene Baker

Illustrations by Richard Wahl

 CHILDRENS PRESS, CHICAGO

Library of Congress Catalog Card Number: 70-182385

1 2 3 4 5 6 7 8 9 10 11 12 13 14 15 16 17 18 19 20 21 22 23 24 25 R 75 74 73 72

"Hey, Craig, look at this!"
Larry said as he turned to his
friend. "Let's try out for our
room Pee Wee team. I would like
to be a good basketball player."

"So would I," said Craig.
"Now we can learn the rules.
Want to shoot some baskets after
school?"

"Good idea," answered Larry.

"Good morning, boys," said
Coach Becker with a smile. The
boys in the gym class smiled, too.
They had looked forward to this
day.

4

"This month we will learn basketball skills," Coach Becker said. "Then we will choose room teams for a Pee Wee contest."

"Basketball can be played by almost everyone. All you need is a strong body and a desire to play. Oh," he laughed, "one other thing is important—good gym shoes!"

"First let us look at this chart of the playing area," said Coach Becker.

"In basketball there are two teams. Each team has five players."

"The object of the game is to score points. A field goal shot through the basket scores two points. A free throw scores one point."

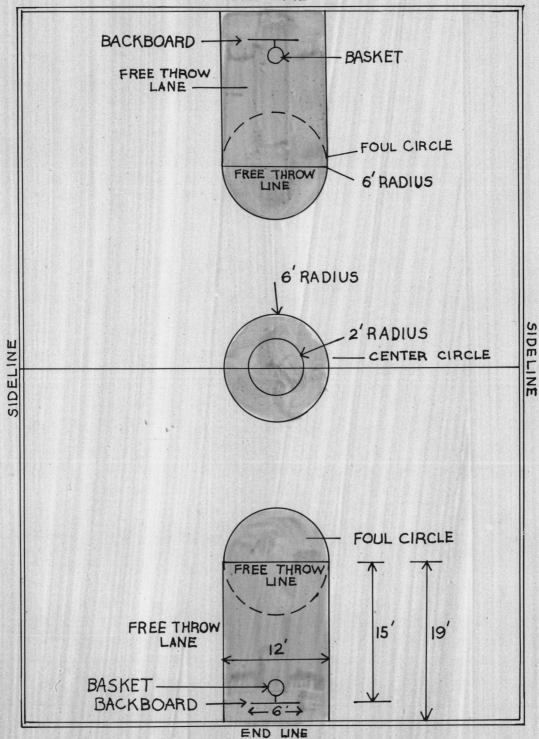

"There are two ways to move the basketball down the court. The ball can be passed or it can be dribbled."

"Line up now, boys. We will have a passing drill."

"This is the *two-hand chest pass*. Keep the ball close to you. Then push with your hands, arms, body, and legs."

TWO - HAND
CHEST PASS

9

"Next we will do the *two-hand bounce pass*. Larry, you bounce the ball off the floor to Bob."

Larry bounced the ball down the gym floor. Bob caught it and bounced it back.

TWO-HAND BOUNCE PASS

OVERHEAD
PASS

"Now the *overhead pass.*
Craig, hold the ball high over
your head. Use your wrists to
throw it."

11

"Good passing, boys! Now
let's try dribbling. To
dribble the ball you bounce
it on the floor as you move."

"Use only the fingertips of
one hand. Don't hold onto the
ball. Keep your knees bent a
little. Hold your other arm
out in front of you."

LOW
DRIBBLE

Each boy took his turn. Down
the floor they went. Coach Becker
watched carefully.

"Practice changing direction.
Stop and start quickly," he called.

Soon the coach blew his whistle.

"Sit down and rest for a while, boys," he said. "Let's talk about basic shots in basketball. Who knows how to do a *two-hand set shot?*"

One boy raised his hand.

"All right, Jack. Place your hands lightly on each side of the ball. Keep your elbows close to your body. Push the ball upward. Keep your eyes on the front rim of the basket."

"Some men who are very good play basketball for money. They learned to play the game when they were your age. They played on high school and college teams."

"Most of them use a *jump shot*. Try a jump shot, Jack. Bend your knees. Push yourself off the floor with both feet. At the top of your jump, push the ball toward the basket. Use your thumb and all four fingers."

JUMP SHOT

Jack took aim. He jumped and shot. *Swish!* The ball went through the basket.

"Nice shot, Jack!" said the coach.

"The last shot we will learn is the *lay-up*," said Coach Becker. "Watch me. I dribble toward the basket. My fingertips push the ball against the backboard. I aim above the basket. When it is done the right way, the ball will touch the backboard. Then it will angle down through the basket."

"All right, everyone. Start shooting," called Coach Becker. He watched each boy carefully. Larry and Craig helped each other.

"You can do it, Craig! Try a jump shot," yelled Larry.

Bob
Jimmy
David
Larry
Jack
Brian
Craig
Paul

After many weeks of practice, Coach Becker said, "You have all tried hard in class. I'm proud of you. Many of you will be good basketball players."

"The following boys are on the Pee Wee team for Miss Hasting's room: Bob . . . Jimmy . . . David . . . Larry . . . Jack . . . Brian . . . Craig . . . Paul. The first game will be next Friday. Miss Hasting's room will play Miss Pelton's room."

Friday's game was exciting. Larry and Craig played most of the game. The score was tied 6 to 6. Larry dribbled the ball down the court. He threw an overhead pass to Craig. Then he ran toward the basket. Craig made a perfect bounce pass to Larry.

"Go into the basket," Larry said quietly to himself. He turned and took a short jump shot.

Swish! It was a perfect shot. The buzzer sounded.

"We win, Larry!" shouted Craig. "The score is 8 to 6!"

That night Larry told his father about the game.

"I'm proud of you, Larry. Knowing you have done well is a good feeling, isn't it?"

"It sure is, Dad. I like basketball a lot. I've decided that I want to be a basketball player."

"Well, son, it's something to think about. To be a good player you must practice a lot."

"It is important to eat the
proper foods. If you don't stay
healthy, you won't have the
strength to play basketball."

"Good grades are also very important. If you don't do well in school you will not be allowed to play on school teams. In fact . . ." Dad paused with a twinkle in his eye. "In fact, I think you'd better start your homework!"

"You're right!" laughed Larry. He picked up his books. As he left the room he was still thinking about that jump shot.

About the author:
Dr. Baker was graduated from Carthage College, Carthage, Illinois. He got his master's degree and doctorate in education at Northwestern University. He has worked as a teacher, as a principal, and as a director of curriculum and instruction. Now he works full time as a curriculum consultant. His practical help to schools where new programs are evolving is sparked with his boundless enthusiasm. He likes to see social studies and language arts taught with countless resources and many books to encourage students to think independently, creatively, and critically. The Bakers, who live in Arlington Heights, Illinois, have a son and two daughters.

About the artist:
Richard Wahl, graduate of the Art Center College of Design in Los Angeles, has illustrated a number of magazine articles and booklets. He is a skilled artist and photographer who advocates realistic interpretations of his subjects. He lives with his wife and small son in Evanston, Illinois.